Abby November, PhD

ARCHWAY
PUBLISHING

Archway Publishing books may be ordered through booksellers or by contacting:

Archway Publishing
1663 Liberty Drive
Bloomington, IN 47403
www.archwaypublishing.com
844-669-3957

ISBN: 978-1-6657-2204-9 (sc)
ISBN: 978-1-6657-2205-6 (e)

Library of Congress Control Number: 2022907558

Print information available on the last page.

Archway Publishing rev. date: 04/19/2022

Contents

Part II
Tales of the Street

Part III
Recipes

Part IV
From this moment: My recipe

PART I

The First Half of My Life

I was born and raised in Brooklyn, even married there. Thereafter I lived in Boston, MA for a year, Providence, RI for three years and Stony Brook, NY for sixteen years. Then on to the Deep South of Athens, GA for five years, two months and fifteen days (but who is counting), Austin in the Great State of Texas for twenty six years and in San Diego, CA for the remainder of my life on this planet.

Introduction

A Legacy is a gift of property, but also anything handed down from the past as from an ancestor or predecessor.

So dear friends and family, if you are reading this, I am not in my physical self - maybe not in my mental one either. But these writings, as primitive as they are, serve as my legacy to you.

Where I came from, the people in my life that mattered, the forces that shaped me physically, emotionally and intellectually will hopefully come across in my stories and poems.

Words are difficult for me, I usually use humor to deflect true, but painful insights.

This doesn't mean a lack of feeling. This doesn't mean humor was used in my early years in Brooklyn, lying dormant through menopause, resurfacing in 1993, when my comedic journey began.

I use it to deflect anger, anxiety and even deepest vulnerability to love.

I only discovered the written word in my seventies, this after my good friend Sandy dragged me to the Older Women's Legacy (OWL) writing group. This event was about six months after my beloved older sister Esty died of ALS.

Etsy lay in the prison of her hospital bed. Tears ran down her cheeks as she struggled to speak with the use of a respirator. Her suffering made me rethink my desire to try everything to stay alive. Waiting for the miracle which never comes. In the past Etsy had prayed to Hashem (Hebrew for God) to take her and spare her beloved grandkinder the agony of seeing her suffer.

My words to you, dear readers, are the following:

Time in this world is short and getting shorter.

Be present. You are here now, so "BE HERE." Enjoy the wind, the smell, the people, make eye contact, not smartphone contact.

Life will never happen quite the same again…ever.

Touch it, taste it, immerse in it, say you are in it. Be there and here, for I will always be a part of you, in the skin, thoughts, feelings, maybe eye color and mannerisms, definitely your DNA. Make the most of it.

Etiology of Bubbe's Desire to be a Bubbe

"When I grow up, I want to be a Bubbe!" – said no one ever, including me, although I loved both Bubbes immensely.

Brooklyn Bubbe was dubbed 'The Bubs'. We lived with her and my Zayde, from the time I was born in 1944 to when she passed in 1963.

Other Brooklyn friends spoke lovingly about their Nonas or Grammys and I had 'The Bubs'. A combination ball buster and Bubbe. Many mornings, as we'd get ready for PS 235, The Bubs would bang on the bathroom door shouting "LET ME IN! I have a weak bladder!" Interesting scene to remember.

I also remember her taking me by subway to see Joseph Schildkraut in 'The Diary of Anne Frank.' Bubs swore to me that Schildkraut was a distance relative of hers. So, as a believing 10-year-old, I wrote a fan letter to him and got nada response. So much for famous relatives.

Bubbe from New Jersey, mom's mother, was an adept seamstress. Originally from Belarus, then a part of Russia, when she emigrated, Bubbe could see a high-end fashion in Bergdorf Goodman or Saks 5th Ave and copy it for her granddaughters. She made all of our dresses for special events, weddings, bar mitzvahs, graduation and first days of school. When my elder sister, Esta, said "I want a dress from Macy's or A&S, not a handmade one," New Jersey Bubbe said, 'That's it!' and we never received another gorgeous homemade item again. Oy vey!

One of the highlights of my life is welcoming each and every one of my grandkinder. Somehow diaper changing grandkids never bothered me the way changing my own two kids' diapers did – long before Pampers!

When the first grandchild was able to identify me, I'd say "Bubbe loves you!" I've even been known to scream it into the pregnant mother's bloated belly.

Maybe a synapse is missing but I've become a card carrying Bubbe, not a GG or Nana. Know what I'm proud of? My title; Dr. Bubbe.

The Beginning

It was a dark and rainy night…oops that's for my Sci-Fi story. My parents, paternal grandparents, and my older sister, who was five years old, lived in an old apartment building at 110 Division Ave. in the Williamsburg section of Brooklyn, many decades before it became fashionable and expensive. It was a two-bedroom, three story walk up. Mom was pregnant with me. The Bubs and Zayde decided it was 'high time' to move into roomier quarters. So the babies didn't share the bathroom with the elders.

My Zayde recounted how the folks moved me in a small baby size bathtub. I think I probably slept in it until I was 12 (hence my short stature and large feet).

My Zayde was my protector and mentor; he always had my back. My elder sister was 'too old' to spend time listening to him, the two little ones were too young to appreciate his anecdotes and astronomy lessons. I was taught the constellations early on, as I sat on our front stoop, he with his unfiltered Camel cigarette, hanging on his lips, me in pigtails, rapt in attention to his tale spilling.

The proceeding stories and poems in this book describe my early family and relationships. I left Brooklyn in the fall of 1964 to attend Beth Israel Hospital Dietetic Internship Program, where I had my first taste of being on my own. The interns had free meals, room, classes. In return we had to work 40-60 hours in all aspects of nutrition, including clinic care, counseling and administration. It was also the mid 60's and the famous 'Boston Strangler' roamed the streets of Boston. The other 12 interns were concerned, but as a fearless (ha ha) New Yorker I said for every BS we have 100 predators in Brooklyn, both the two and four footed variety.

My fiancé was an economics Ph.D. student at Brown University, about an hour away. My parents thought that 'Boston was sufficiently far from

Providence, so I didn't need the safe sex lecture, although Mom once said "Better my daughter be dead than pregnant out of wedlock". Oy vey, my sex life was tainted from the get go.

My college years were at Hunter College when the Park Ave campus was for girls only. My locker mate introduced me to her fiancé's BFF and it was love at first, smell…I mean sight. I loved the smell of his after shave lotion mixed with Johnson & Johnson's baby powder. He also gave great phone! I fell in lust with the deep resonant sound of his voice on the phone.

The only off putting moment was when I asked "what is that noise and who is screaming I AM NOT ROCKEFELLOW." It was his mother telling him to stop talking and running up the phone bill. This was 50+ years prior the age of cellphones..

We married after dating five 5 yrs. We lived an academic life.

His 50-year career involved teaching, research and department chairmanships at three major universities. I worked as a consultant dietitian. And along the way, earned a MS in Human Nutrition at University of Wisconsin - Madison and a Ph.D. in Nutrition at NYU, while helping to raise two incredibly attractive, brilliant and talented children.

These two, Eric and Deb, have between them four incredibly attractive, brilliant and talented kinder. I say they all take after me (LMAO).

The purpose of these pages is to edify, identify and horrify,(oops, illustrate) why I am the way I am.

Hoping as you read on, that you realize the deep caring and love I have for you, which may or may not have not been demonstrated or felt by you.

Lovingly signed,

Abby, Mom (mostly Bubbe) aka Abby November

Zayde's Words

People have mottos to live by, daily affirmations, like the Serenity Prayer from the 12-step program. My Zayde was the smartest man I've ever known. Self-educated, he never graduated high school. Zayde grew up in a brick tenement on the lower east side of New York City. The eldest of eight kids, he adored his overworked, prematurely-aged mother, Esther, and feared his rigid religious father.

Zayde worked selling apples, newspapers, bagels, whatever he could obtain to help the family. His religious dad was always in the temple praying, learning or schmoozing with his bearded pals. His mother took in wash. Zayde described the clean washed clothes strung up on clothing lines between tenements.

He was able to work for the United States Post Office and by the time he married at age 20, had enough money to rent a one-bedroom apartment in Brooklyn. He was proud of his paycheck, pension and benefits, meaning his wife Bertha never had to work, like his mother.

My dad, Sidney, Zayde's only child, married at 21. Dad and Mom squeezed into the living room of the tiny apartment. For several years the four of them along with my sister were squished together until I was born. Then my grandparents and parents put a down payment on a real three level brick house in the East Flatbush section of Brooklyn in the late 1940s.

No one bought things "on time". Zayde said if you can't afford it, you don't need it. Cash was king. I was Zayde's favorite as I most reminded him of his beloved mother. She, like me, was quick with a joke or a silly name for silly neighbors. He was my best friend and the only one at the house who gave me unconditional love.

When I was jealous of a rich classmate who had matching bedroom furniture, bedding and even draperies, Zayde would ask, "do you think that would make you happier than when we go to Crazy Joe's candy shop for an egg cream or when we sit on the stoop and see the stars and I name the constellations for you?" I had to admit he was right.

He brought home from little gifts for me from the Grand Central Post Office. My favorite was Mallomars (chocolate-covered marshmallow graham crackers). Once he brought me an almost life-sized (to me) doll, dressed as a little Dutch girl complete with yellow woolen winged pigtails. I had to share her with my baby sister. Whenever I bemoaned not having a new dress or shoes like my classmates had, he'd say "it is what it is; sometimes you're up and sometimes you're down." I remember his words as I ponder its truthfulness. Happiness is not things: it is experiences with people you love and who love you. It is shared egg creams, Mallowmars and sitting on the stoop staring at the stars on a cool Brooklyn night and learning about the constellations and wondering again about what is happening on those stars and who are those people, and Zayde saying, "It is what it is."

Stars Over Brooklyn

So there we are, Zayde, The Bubs, my parents, my older sister, my baby sister and me – all sharing our two-story, three-bedroom home. There were no trees growing near our concrete yard. On the weekdays Zayde took the subway to his job at the Grand Central Station post office.

Summer evenings were spent on our red brick front porch. Looking back, I remember Zayde and me enjoying the cooler evening breezes and him pointing out the constellations, the stars and heavenly bodies. I didn't understand a lot of it, but I loved being the one sitting with Zayde on the green metal rusted porch chairs. Esta was fourteen and too interested in boys to spend 'boring' time with an old man. Margie at four always seemed to be into everything, and the baby, the male heir Stephen, was in diapers. We had a black and white TV which could be heard outside on the porch through the broken window screens and screen door.

My mother, father, and The Bubs sat in the semi-darkened room staring at the little set, lost in Uncle Milty and Lawrence Welk. Zayde and I thought the visible sky more entertaining than Uncle Milty in drag.

Holiday and birthday gifts were eagerly anticipated, but I cannot remember them. What I do remember is simply the image of a pigtailed girl hanging on every word of wisdom from the mouth of her beloved Zayde.

Decades have passed. I have a granddaughter of my own. Will she remember the dolls or toys I gave her? Or will she remember my stories of her mother's early life, her grandma's prior life, or the days we spent sitting in the Colorado summer grass telling stories, chasing butterflies?

Will she ask me if the stars over Boulder are the same stars I saw with my Zayde? And If so, which ones are they? Perhaps she'll remember the stars and not the toys.

Here's to The One

Who taught me to plant potatoes and corn
On a confiscated Brooklyn vacant lot
Who left our home daily to work the graveyard shift at Central Post Office
Who brought us four candy and treats

Spoiling us and lifting our spirits in an otherwise grey overcast Household
Here's to the one who held my hand telling stories of tenement life
In the crowded lower east side
Who loved his mother despised and fear his
Father who claimed to see the face of God
But emotionally abused his overworked wife and
Ignored his 7 children except to upbraid them for disrespect
Zayde, how I still see him in suspenders-held old pants soil stained holding a shovel
Smashed brimmed hat to shade his eyes as he and I labored at weed pulling
Here's to Zayde dressed in a white kittle* leading the sedar, the four of us opening the door for the angel
Zayde laboriously clipping his wife's toughened yellow toenails
Here is to the one we went hand in hand to Crazy Joes for his smokes and shared our egg cream.
Here is to my Zayde carried in the ambulance after a stroke, here's to the slamming of its cold metal door.
Here's to the one to whom I never said goodbye

---

*   Kittle = Fringed prayer shawl

Kosher Trash of Brooklyn

When I grew up
There was no grass, flowers or trees
Brick and concrete
were on my street
But another world only a bus away was
Prospect Park, with trees, flowers and lake
Ducks, squirrels, boats to take.
Where I grew up
Brick and concrete
Trolley car rumbles down the street
Buses billowing smoke down the street
There are no trees on my street
When I grew up,
Hand me down clothes were a treat, one pair of shoes a year
Feet, make them last
When I grew up
We played stoop ball, hide and seek
on our brick and concrete street
Big sister and I shared a bed
Family of 8 we shared a toilet
Yet I never thought we were poor
On our street of brick and concrete

Growing Up November

Brooklyn house, its decay
Matched my teeth
Dad said if not in front, just pull it
Mom clinically depressed whole life
Told me her mom loved Muriel more
'cause Muriel was little and blonde
Skinny women are mean
Girls can't be doctors
Once you're married, don't complain to me
You made your bed, you lie in it
What do I want to be when I grow up?
Best memories are of my grandkinder
Our kids early years – Bar & Bat Mitzvah
Old friends – NY, Athens, TX, SD
Close relatives my Zayde, Bubs???
Aunt Muriel: never got to say goodbye to her mind.
But, her body survived another 8yrs
Old George from the Bronx called him every Sunday
Missed one Sunday
He never spoke with me again. I was eight years old. Old George from
The Bronx
Lived on the third floor no elevator, drank beer on fire escape and threw
bottle down the alley. Odd, he never hit a soul.
Aunt Mary and our Uncle Abe
He ate graham crackers and warm milk; probably had an undiagnosed
ulcer
Childless Mary gave parenting advice and criticism to mom
If it was negative, mom absorbed it for she had a magnet for hurts, arrows
and guilt

There was no industrial sized Prozac, the but there was Jack Daniels
The bottle at bedside…for medicinal use only, she said.

I miss them all, and when leaving the vestibule, we call life, entering
'The World Beyond' will I see them?
Or is this reality all written from the ashes of our grandparent's shells
and asphalt of the Lower East Side?

Basketball

In the Brooklyn spring of 1957, G. Wingate High School was tough enough without missing a school day. My shoulder was killing me, probably from an old basketball injury. Physical Education (P.E.) was required. Most junior high and high schools had swimming pools, allowing kids to fulfil their requirement in a heated pool. Wingate High School had no pool. We were forced to partake in volleyball, basketball and other herculean sports.

I had the distinction of being the shortest girl in my grade's P.E. class. My cohorts all towered over me. I remember being last chosen for the basketball team. As I raced to get the ball, another girl bumped into my arm and I felt a rather hard crack. Despite the ice and the aspirin, the pain got worse. Soon, I was medically excused and 'benched'.

Kids can be cruel, and words can hurt. As I walked through the cafeteria wearing a sling, my ex-best friend Lyn said in a stage whisper, "there she goes, Miss Social Flop!"

In addition to the embarrassment, the steady numbness, lack of movement and pain continued. Doctors through I had developed juvenile arthritis.

After one of my numerous x-rays, Dr. Greenberg spoke quietly to my father. Of course, I was not told what he said. So, when my parents took me to the Joint Disease hospital in New York City, I thought it was an ordinary doctor or therapy visit. Imagine my shock to find out I was scheduled for immediate surgery.

Dr. Joseph Buchman was assigned to my case. I call him Dr. B. He explained that I had a bone tumor, not arthritis. First, he wanted to biopsy the tumor and depending upon the type, I may or may not have an arm.

I woke up with both arms and saw my dad cry for the first time in my life.

The Door Slammed

I was twelve years old. The Brooklyn sky was grey, the sun hadn't visited our street for weeks.

The leaves were gone, and a chilly gloom settled upon us as we got ready to burrow in for the winter months. Zayde had been acting weird in the past weeks. He seemed agitated and he really missed his job at the Post Office. He was forced to take retirement at age 67 and missed the working, smoking, drinking and schmoozing that went on during the graveyard shift. Besides, he secretly told me, being home fulltime with your grandma, "The Bubs", was making him nuts!

Zayde used to take me for walks to the candy store, dubbed 'Crazy Joe's. He would buy Camel cigarettes with no filters and get me an egg cream for a nickel. What a special treat, just Zayde and myself. The other three siblings were not interested in spending time with 'an old man' or were still in diapers. Often, I would wait for Zayde after school.

I remember trying to stuff my hands into my peacoat pockets for warmth, but they had holes in them. My mom would be annoyed that my gloves needed repair again. I was not competent enough to do it myself, so it fell on her.

I waited for Zayde for our walk to Crazy Joe's. I told The Bubs and my parents, "this is not right, he's always here to walk me." When darkness fell at 5:00 P.M., a police car came to our house with Zayde in it.

He was found confused and wandering the neighborhood but was able to state his name.

There was a conference between my folks, the police and The Bubs resulting in a call to our family doctor. Seemingly, within minutes, an ambulance arrived from the local hospital.

I watched from the creepy darkness of my parents' bedroom window ledge as drivers gently put Zayde in the back of the ambulance. My thoughts begged him to look up, turn, wave…anything.

The door slammed. I never saw Zayde again, nor said goodbye.

The Bullet

While I was living in Georgia, Mom said, 'If I lose my ability to think, put a bullet through my head.' My siblings and I ignored her words.

Later that year she was scheduled for triple bypass surgery. She was very anxious.

Dad was uncomfortable in a role of caregiver. My elder sister lived near their apartment, but was unavailable, leaving my brother, other sister, and me to 'parent' from afar.

After the bypass surgery, mom suffered a stroke while in the hospital. I remember the impotence I felt as I sat bedside holding her hand as she cried for 'Momma.' I asked the nurse to page her doctor to which the nurse replied, "use the payphone, its faster."

We were in a major teaching hospital and expected at least courteous service. We were sadly mistaken.

Eventually her condition allowed her to be discharged. She refused the rehab center saying, "they will harvest my organs for sale." Was this a sign of incompetency or too many science fiction books? My elder sister and dad did agree that the best place for her was home! Oy Vey! My dad was her fulltime caregiver. A practical nurse came twice within the first week to change dressings and check vital signs.

During this time I called daily. Our conversations were monosyllabic and occasionally if she spoke a sentence it was confused, i.e. "my shoes hurt." She had no shoes on, she meant "feet."

One afternoon, Dad called me and said, "Tell her to eat! She's not eating or drinking." I told her to have some oatmeal, toast and tea, which were her favorite foods.

She parroted "hot tea," and those were the last words she ever spoke to me.

Dad said she's slipping off the bed.

"Dad! Call 911!" I said. She lapsed into a coma. I flew up to New York to say goodbye before she died.

I was cleaning the apartment and I found many un-swallowed pills under her pillow on the couch.

She made her own "bullet." She did it "her way."

Early November Health Habits

Imaginary fears were a specialty of mother November. For her worrying was hard work. Dad often said she awakened and worried if things were "too right." The Evil Eye (Yoseh Horah) would bite our tush (butt).

To avoid Polio, my parents had us avoid water. To be safe, the November family stayed away from beaches, pools, even bathtubs, as much as possible. We did save the hot bath water for the next kid before it cooled. I remember getting the Salk vaccine in school. It was not uncommon to see kids in leg braces back then. Now, it's rare to see children with leg braces, but common to see kids with orthodontic braces.

"Schnapps" were always present in our household, used as medicine. Mom would keep a bottle of Jack Daniels at bedside for a night cap or sleeping aide. My Bubbe was known to take an afternoon nip for "poor blood." The November family believed a "clean colon" is a healthy colon. Therefore, when ill, an enema can't hurt. Tonics, worry, prayer and enemas gave mother November a feeling of control in an uncertain world.

Christmas gifts of Schnapps, Jack Daniels and Johnnie Walker were commonplace. The kids would be given some Schnapps in orange juice or tea to cure the "chills" and prevent colds. As well as wearing garlic to keep away germs…and vampires. It worked; we were never bitten by a vampire.

Mom's Life Lessons

Smile and praise him
Let him win in tennis
Always defer to his movie choices
Smile and praise him
Girls are not doctors
Be a teacher maybe a nurse
Don't show off your brains
Smile and praise him
My lobotomy took
I blew my own horn
He smiles and listens
I am my own person
I smile when saying, no, you are wrong
I win at poker and tennis
I became a doctor

Ode to My Zayde

"You are my sunshine," he sang to me!
I was his favorite
"My only sunshine"
He loved me without strings
"When skies are sunny or blue"
Made me happy by his smile
"When skies are cloudy and gray"
Gave me laughter and candy
He'll never know how much I love him
Until the hospital took my sunshine away.
I never had my sunshine again

Esta's Words

My childhood Girl Scout troop attended the Nutcracker ballet at the New York City Ballet Center. It was magical. We rode the rumbling, smokey subway into the bowels of the East River tunnel until we arrived in the Big Apple, then we walked uptown to the ballet. I never thought that humans could be so delicate, graceful, and controlled. I couldn't wait to tell my grandmother mother, and sisters about the magical show. The men in the family were either too old, too busy, or in diapers. I told my mom, "I want to be a ballerina" to which she replied, "you're a klutz. Besides, you have piano legs like cousin Francie."

Funny, since all the women in my family have big feet, legs, and big mouths. Thus, my career ended before it started! I spent the remainder of the day buried in my pillow on the bed I shared with my older sister, Esta.

Esta patted me, and said, "there are many graceful things in the world, besides a ballerina."

"Can I wear a tutu?" I replied

"No," she said, "but beauty and grace surround us even in Brooklyn. Go with Daddy to the Botanical Gardens where he takes photographs of the lovely birds and butterflies. Watch their wings and flight. See how the flowers sway in the breeze."

Esta's words made me experience the natural grace around us. She was a painter and captured the color of beauty and movement. She didn't dance or soar, but she found grace in her moments of prayer. As she lay dying of ALS she illustrated the ultimate level of grace as she accepted God's plan for her and welcomed her to the next world.

Sweet Face

My sister Esta's voice is my own. We have strong Brooklyn accents. People often mistook my phone voice for Esta's.

Five years my senior, Esta was a gifted artist. She saw the world in a wild palette of vibrant colors, not the black, white and gray of our daily lives.

She was awarded scholarships to the Brooklyn Museum and Fashion Institute of Technology.

She fell in love with a tall, dark and handsome, but abusive man. His voice became hers. Her five children became a vibrant palette.

Her view of God's lovely colors was marred by the black, blue and purple masks on her skin. "I'm clumsy, always walking into things," she'd say.

She twice ran away and left him for good after about twenty years of marriage. Free from him, Esta would call me weekly, asking for "my little Zeiskeit (sweet face)." These were happy years for her, filled with friends, travel and family. She made art, handmade cards for any occasion. Filled with her love of freedom and colors, her cards were gifts to us. She taught arts and crafts to the elderly at the Jewish Center. Her prayer book was her constant companion.

Then ALS stole her body, but not her spirit.

She said, "Abby, this is not the only world"

July Fourth, Esta's voice was stilled

I long for the phone call asking for "My Zeiskeit."

I miss her.

Untaught

How can I say thanks for the lessons you taught?
No, I didn't need them as a pig tailed brat
Nor as a semi formed woman
Half century past and learning survived.
But still deaf eyes and clouded ears cannot hear my thanks
From the simple lessons of always wearing clean underwear
"Just in case"
To always eating breakfast and saying nightly prayers
The primal lesson not taught to say I love you and thank you
We're not taught
Before you vanished in the mist of my life

Wedding Night Lesson

On the eve of my wedding
Marriage is not 50/50 said my mom
It's not even 60/40
Sometimes it's not even fair.
Thanks a lot mom, depressing words.
I want to share down the middle!
"Fair is fair," I screamed.
But when we swear to take each other in sickness and in health,
For richer or for poorer,
These are not promised future facts.
Will you be there when my limbs and brain are weak?
Can I be there for you when your mind and eyes dim?
Fair is fair: How childlike I was 50 years past.
Got it straight- Marriage is not fair.
Nor is life.

Last Words Spoken

Last words spoken to me by loved ones before entering the next world

I admonished Mom to drink or eat as her health was failing, her last words to me were "Hot tea."
Dad's surgery for colon cancer, laughingly said, "I passed gas."

My grandma, The Bubs, said, "Never tell people your weight, they'll be jealous."

My beautiful older sister before she was put on a ventilator and succumbed to ALS; "always remember this is just a vestibule to a better place."

My Zayde, "remember you are my sunshine, my only sunshine."

Uncle Mike on the phone from the hospital days before dying, "It is what it is."

But not one said, "I love you, be yourself, no regrets, we'll meet again."

The Tempest

Dark clouds, thunder and lightning smash within my skull.

My heart beats in time to the thunder

Lightening sizzled in the sky,

Bolts of it thrown from some watching angry deity

Laughing silently at my discomfort

Squirrels scurry nonstop, owls screeching at the silvery snatches of light,

Kasha, my Golden, on the cool tile floor shivering and moaning

I lie down beside her and hold her close, feeling her warm dog breath on my cheek. We shake no more.

Sun fights through the clouds and cobwebs of my mind

Squirrels and owls cease their screeching

Respite at last:

We are calm

Lies My Mother Told Me

"When you eat in the dark while standing, you don't gain weight."

"Always spoil your husband or a skinny bitch will steal him."

"Don't trust anyone with a flat tush."

These guidelines resonated with me and my sisters for decades. One sister stayed with an abusive man for decades, because "better a bad marriage than no marriage!"

My younger sister and I didn't drink all of Mom's Kool-Aid, but we did believe that a fat woman is not selfish and that she always puts the needs of family before her own. Hence, the not trusting a flat tush.

Years of life experience, therapy and leaving mom's gravitational pull enabled us to gain clearer insight on the Truth. The myths mom believed were her own insecurities, fears and low self-esteem – a fear of the world in general and losing her "trophy," in her mind, husband specifically. Dad was present physically, but not emotionally. He was more involved with his hobbies du jour than even his job or kids. He was often "between jobs" and mom was the main provider.

After 50 years of living and loving all types of tushes, I learned that one judges another by the content of their soul and heart, not by the contour of their tush.

Funnel Clouds

Spending over twenty years of my life in the Northeast, I experienced a variety of Mother Nature's acts: hurricanes, blizzards, and heat waves.

Nothing prepared me for a move to Madison, Wisconsin in the mid-1970s. I read The Wizard of Oz as a kid and to my kids. The thought of a funnel cloud developing into a powerful tornado picking people up and placing them somewhere else was a fabrication. Impossible to imagine a storm of this magnitude able to lift up roof tops, cars, mega trees and transport them miles away. To me it was an exaggeration, a myth.

I was in a Master's Program at University of Wisconsin. Driving back and forth was no big deal in rain or snow flurries. I grew up driving on rainy and snowy roads. Cold was another thing. By October, I was wearing my full allotment of warm clothes. Long thermal underwear, old lady granny panties underneath. Then outer layers of wool slacks, turtlenecks and crew sweaters. Topped by down coats, hat, scarves and mittens. That was just me. I had to get a four and six-year-old to undergo the same time-consuming process.

We were driving home from shopping one evening when we heard the sirens proclaim tornado warning. We kept driving, hoping it was a test. I was scared and excited. Afraid of the stories of our car being lifted by a giant hand and carelessly thrown around, yet excited to check the validity of the myth. Looking out the rear car window, I saw a funnel cloud following us. It touched down far behind us. We sped up and drove as close to the side of the road wall as possible and stopped. We waited. We felt the little Ford Pinto tremble. No one spoke for what seemed like minutes but was probably seconds. Trembling, we looked behind us. To one side roofs had vanished, trees were uprooted; our side was untouched. We restarted the car, drove home, knowing that we could add tornado to our list of adventures. Indeed, this myth is a reality.

Life in The Slow Lane

1982 was spent in the magical city of Perth, on the west of coast of Australia. The fauna and flora were strange and exotic. We arrived in July, after the end of the kid's middle school spring semester. It was fall down under and the school year was about to begin. My "poor" kids had no summer break! They were griping. Until they realized that school in the Land of Oz is different. Our son took no books to school, carrying instead a footy (Australian football) under his arm and a tennis racket. Perth's schools encouraged sports. My kids' summer adventure turned into a fall one. They learned that the English language in Australia was a bit strange, having unusual words and idioms. For example: lollis meant candy, a jumper is a sweater, the boot of a car is its trunk, a 'wog' is a bug or germ, commonly known as the common cold, to be 'crook' is to be sick.

Funny words aside, the people were friendly. Strangers frequently invited us over for a "cuppa (coffee or tea)." Unlike the New Yorkers' half-hearted non-committal "let's do lunch soon," in Perth this meant tomorrow. They called you when you did not show up. Australia was populated by immigrants, the native aboriginals and in Sydney, descendants of an original criminal colony sent from the United Kingdom.

Life in the 1980s was a slower, more pleasant pace. Sport was encouraged. Work ethic and individuality inherent in jobs and education, but time for a cuppa superseded work time. I was teaching dietetics at the West Australian Institute of Technology. Students were very polite and respectful unlike my students at SUNY - Stony Brook. Every week we'd drive (on the left, oops-wrong side of road). We'd go up the west coast to be near the incredible emerald Indian Ocean. It is a breathtaking coastline. We took a hydrofoil to Rottnest Island with the kids, rented bikes and explored. We got to see the Quokkas - miniature marsupials in their natural habitat. Kindness to strangers was a fact of life since residents we met were all once "strangers in a strange new land." Aside from the incredible vistas and animals, Perth reminded me of the United States in the 1950's – safe to leave doors unlocked, able to drop in on neighbors, and loyalty to family, God, and nation, some of which I feel is lacking in present day United States.

Lovely plants and furry little koalas (aka stoners) abounded, as did the not so cute Tasmanian Devils and a vast array of poisonous snakes and spiders. Friendly neighbors, always eager to help us out, were much appreciated. Yes, the language was the same but the local customs and pace of life were pleasantly different.

It was a wonderful sense of freedom, not to be on the clock, not to be a human doing but a human "being." I learned that savoring a cuppa is a relaxing tradition. Which we in the United States, land of hurry sickness, sorely needed.

Dropping in unannounced on neighbors, a tradition back from 50's, when doors were not locked and friends and neighbors were welcomed to drop by for a cuppa and a chat.

We were not at that time a high-tech, low touch society. It was acceptable to hug a neighbor's child or a senior citizen and not be labeled a pervert; being neighborly was encouraged.

I remember the 50's when neighbors looked out on your comings and goings. Some may ascribe a nosiness to this, I felt a sense of safety in the knowledge. I could run next door to Mrs. Goldberg or McCoy for a scraped knee, tissue for a running nose or reassurance that mom was in route.

How I long to return to the serene beauty and rugged coastline of the Indian Ocean where neighbors drop in and doors are not locked. I fear though that the decades have eroded the feelings of safety and neighborliness.

Sunshine

Sam's four-year-old frail body
Rarely escaped from its metal encasement:
Wheelchair holds her stick legs, encased in braces
A new therapist came today
Helping her out of her iron and steel claws,
Sat her on ground near an open door
She butt-scooted to the yard and sat in the sun, looking up and smiling
Sam's face was a big smile like an opening sunflower.
Then her savior did something new:
Stood her up supporting her shoulders.
Smiles all around at the sun, at the friends, and her savior
How little it took to get that smile: seeing the sun and standing
Wouldn't it be great if we all could appreciate life's miracles?
Ability to stand and have sunshine fill your soul.

The Boogeyman

Black straight hair framing round perfect face. Child of delight, a squeal, a hug
Who grows up too sweet, too gentle
Gentle Bear
He's a clown and
Afraid of the dark, of loud noises, mean spirited faces.
Learned to hide thoughts and feelings by
Magical thinking & imaginary friends, "Jinko" did it
"Jinko" will be there to clean up the mess,
Why the need to open closet doors to scare out boogeyman.
They never really leave us,
For they shapeshift into new our worlds
We open doors and windows for the light and air – but still the eyes always follow.
Chattering monkeys of his youth, stuck in the branches of his mind
Boogeyman follow you from daytime,
Lurking in the alleyways and doorways of our soul,
Into the night mists of our dreams, ever waiting to leap and maul.
To inject venom of loss and hate.
An Armani suit and Rolex cannot shield you
Nor can a packed wallet with green flesh
How do we kill a Boogeyman?
Face it with your head held high, a baseball bat, and a welder's metal mask.
You may huff and puff, blow and bluster, but you are but dust and ashes
And he will always be …he….

Autumn Dreams

Gold, red, green, and orange
Feathers from God
Crip, cold, burnt

Apple, leaves, flavors

Hot summer shimmery sun fades slowly into

Smells of frost, rustle of dry, crisp leaves
Gone to return to mother...to be
Rebirthed again from her warm womb

Festival of Lights

An eon ago
Warriors of destruction
Hate of a people faced destruction
A bit of oil
Candelabra in a temple
Light for one night only
Miracle of lights, oil burned eight days and nights
For brightening their souls, feeling hearts with freedom
People of the book, keeper of the flame,
As we join our ancestors by lighting the candles with our children
As we are instructed by our parents and grandparents
A bit of oil, miracle and light, we are surrounded by flickering our past
Ancestors upon shoulders of their ancestors
For so it goes forever forward

Dark Cloud

Bright brown eyes
Indian dark straight hair framed a cherub.
Quietly playing with his Legos
Hopeful expectant, enjoying friends
Loving his Bubbe and Zayde
Enjoying his food
Enjoying special T.V.
Bedtime stories ready by his dad

Eventually accepting the newborn girl interloper
Although he tried to smother her once and admonished me to 'hit baby
with hammer'
Good at math, puzzles logistics
Not a kvetch
Where did the dark cloud come from

Mea culpa I worked.
I was too busy, too impatient
Wasn't there mentally or physically when I should have been.
Dark cloud often hidden by sunshine, at a ballgame, or a trip
Stormy weather repeats, life not worth living
Is it because not loved enough, not hugged enough
I wait for the phone to alarm us through the night
He's alone
Engulfed and alive, wandering, through the darkness

The Substitute

As I was wheeled toward the operating room, Mom bent over and kissed me. Her eyes were red. She was crying, But why? She had promised me, "It's just a little nothing. He'll take it out". Next, I remember seeing white gowned, ghost like people, bright lights, and then a mask going over my nose and mouth. A voice said, "count backwards from 100." I think I made is to 94, yet the ether smell sticks to my nasal passages to this day.

What a bummer of a summer for anyone, especially a fourteen-year-old nerdy kid from Brooklyn. The doctor who has been treating me for juvenile arthritis with hydrotherapy, massage and chicken soup, clearly saw that a bone tumor has developed and now engulfed the head of the humorous, after the twentieth x-ray. It wasn't funny! This was a sarcoma, a malignant rapidly growing bone cancer necessitating amputation.

Both parents were with me at the New York Hospital for Joint Diseases. I had never seen my dad cry; now his eyes were red rimmed. He claimed to have a cold! Dad worried? No, he was perennial Peter Pan who never matured. Yet if he was frightened for me, I knew I should be also.

A new Chief Resident was introduced to us. Dr. B. who explained that he was a last-minute substitute for my regular surgeon who'd had a personal emergency. In the midst of surgery, Dr. B. insisted on waiting for the frozen section before amputation: "you can cut later." The results were benign. Even with all the physical signs and symptoms, the x-ray history, they were wrong. My arm and I are still together. Dr. B. scheduled a second surgery for the next week and all the tumor was removed. Even with the ugly scars and limited range of motion, I'm alive and have both arms. I had to have a bone graft from my pelvis to fill in the void left by the tumor.

A substitute doctor I'd never met, and a last-minute cancellation made such a difference in my life.

Dreams Can Come True

Still Me..[*]
Wishes and dreams of winning the trophy:
Of the most applause, laughter, and cheers.
It's the dream of every comedienne:
Acceptance, prizes and crowd's screams;
Flying high in the moment:
without chemistry- I'm in the zone
We are one in the light.
The audience loved me:
I won the ruby Chalice, the golden slipper
and big prize.
I got the Brass ring of Comedy
But nothing changed
I am still me:
Wrinkles, sags and achy joints.

---

[*]   After winning "King of the Stage," Comedy Palace, San Diego, October 3, 2017.

Upon Visiting Aunt with Alzheimer's

I see old photos
You are there smiling now, too you are here, smiling
But you're not here
You do not see me; your eyes look but can't see my sad smile
You do not know my face
You hear my voice but don't know my words
How can you not be you?

Conundrum

Abrupt, angry and impatient are you.
Why, what did I do? I ask, in my mind and out my mouth.
Instead of what the hell is going on?
Or was it me?
Oy, what did I do?
Is it pain, terror in the news?
Childhood woes revisited?
Words like poison arrows flung at me,
Never to be removed
Pinch and probe to my soul.
Or are we two people in one body;
Fighting pushing forward and backward, hurting and loving.
Or is it plaques and tangles of your brain?
Congested like the Los Angeles freeway
Taking the person I loved further away?

Alone

In the middle... alone.
Subways at rush hour body to body;
I'm alone, no one sees me, yet I feel their breath.
I am an island in jet stream of mossy seaweed.
Surrounded by gazillions: exposed, naked, but no one sees me.

My hand is open and no one takes it.
Surrounded by love and warmth
I'm cold and alone.
Do I have a repel aura or odor?

Why don't they see me, feel me, hear me?
Alone in a crowd, I will vaporize into
More nothingness that never was.

Pill Boxes

My Pill Boxes
Every week I fill them
For A.M and P.M.
Weeks fly like pages on a calendar;
So every two weeks I refill them
For A.M and P.M.
But in two weeks, they disperse like sand grains in a bottle
So where do these moments go?
So now, every month I refill them
For A.M and P.M.
But they dissipate like the steam a raindrop makes on the hot cement
I trapped them in the box
So now I refill them monthly
For A.M. and P.M.
Tried Velcro on the lid
And yet, they vanish almost before
I close the lid.
Where is their vapor, their trail?
Can I ever fill them just so?
The world slows enough for me
To breathe
between the refills
For the A.M. and P.M.
And in the living

Ouch

My heart hurts
Where your words cut into it
Bleeding, tender, jagged
Words like pointed poisoned pens
Stung worse than a root canal
Cut deeper than a carving knife
Depth of which can't be mended glued or
Healed
Can't be forgotten, can be forgiven
But why?

Rocks

The red rock
I collect rocks from places I visit.
Proudly displayed in my home except the red stone.
Worn by nature, torn by man
Battered by nature, tormented by man
Sun baked color, man-made horror shaded its crust
Not a particularly lovely stone
Not smooth, but prickly, painful, dark stained
I put in my hand:
It felt warm to the touch
Needles prodded my skin
My palm felt the screams of pain.
A dark but silent cry whispered at me
Too terrible to display or praise
I save it in a kept in a dark box
Lest it diminishes the glow of the others
The rock was found at the entrance to Auschwitz.
It was probably trod upon decades ago by the 6 million
Including my lost family
Their tears and blood washing over its roughness,
Never again.

Pain

no blood or cuts
yet irreparable wound
deeper and deadlier than a sharp knife
no first aide or band aide or
kiss the booboo will help
the depth and strength of the hidden wound
intakes the statue of Liberty a tinker toy
the rock in my heart harder and lower
no modern drug will ever dissolve it.
Words spoken hang like poison crystals in the air between us
Never to melt, diminish or forgotten
forgiven, …maybe, but, forgotten… never.

Redux

Would u do it again?
The pain the tears
The love the joy
Would you? Could you,
Knowing our winged words wound.
But learning warm hugs heal
Would you. Could you.
I would, to gaze into your eyes and see your bright brown eyes with love,
just as I've glared into your face and seen distain and impatience.
That said, the 'yes I would 'stands now and for eternity.
If there is a hereafter: I will find you.

CIS: Confinement Insanity Syndrome

I tested positive for CIS:
Locked down and locked in: Confined House Arrest.

Masked Faces now mandated: breathing hard through paper, cloth or vinyl
No hugging or touching – social distance.
Watch your wanton glances: look from six feet.
When will normal resume? Or is it gone?

I remember crowds, subway hangers, shaking hands. How I miss how and crave the touch and hugs of friends, is this the new normal?

Tons of sprays alcohol – Purell
Did I get the germs?
Maybe lurking on my mail, my groceries. Or on my face. I am forbidden to touch my face.

Drinking wine earlier and earlier, eating to fill the void
Never filling the void except with solitude and more damn quiet.

Nine Weeks of Getting Greyer, Fatter and More Frightened

I never thought of myself as old, maybe older.
Well, maybe when my grandson asks me "When I get OLD like you..."
Does he see me as one foot in the grave, the other on a banana peel?
"When you were my age [10], did you have TV or telephone?", he asks
I'd laugh and cuddle him, as big as he is, on my ample lap. Now we're
1000 miles away

Now all I can do is kiss my phone and touch his virtual curls with my
hand – not exactly touchy feely.
Now I've washed my hands so much, I do it in my sleep – or so my
bedmate tells me. 'You are counting slowly to twenty and shaking your
hands.' Oy vey! What is the new normal?

Stacks of tissues, rolls of toilet paper, bags of flour, gallons of water and
the PILLS. PILLS for everything and anything! Plastic gloves and masks
and it's not even Halloween.

Friends disappear under masks, hats and scarves. I've discovered alcohol-
based hand sanitizer, I made my own with 70 proof. Do you know
alcohol is in my morning Bloody Marys, Bushmills and in my evening
Irish coffee?

Be sanitized inside and out. No place to hide, nowhere is safe, nine weeks
so far of fright, fear, grayer, fatter and fully sanitized.

Marriage Wisdom

Mom told me it's not fifty-fifty or seventy-thirty
Always give 100 percent and expect nothing.
You will always be surprised by the unexpected.
Bring small gifts, like a single perfect rose, like her
Major goof, an extra-large anything…or a nosehair clipper.
A friend was giving advice to a newly wed guy
Be loving and respectful
Faithful in your heart, avoid lusting in your mind.
Don't criticize her family or her fur baby.
Most of all, remember three words she wants to hear most:
"You're right, dear!"

Some Enchanted Evening

I saw you across a crowded bowling alley
I watched your handsome face
Across a crowded room
Saw no other face in that room.
We were strangers when we met
So long ago in a stranger's home.
Once I saw you, no eyes for another
Across the crowded room
Once I looked into your brown eyes, we were strangers no more.
For I cling to your heart and soul.
I've never let you go
Though the years have slowed our steps and greyed our hair;
We have shared tears of joy and of sorrow.
Your crooked smile remains in my heart
Its warm touch melts me…
Strangers no more..

55th Anniversary

Here's a salute to the guy who taught me to drive…oy vey,
To the brown-eyed teach who gave me a B in
Statistics for Dummies,
Even though I was in the top 1% of his class
To the fellow who holds me up when I falter, kicks my butt when I
kvetch,
Checks my grammar, gives me straight answers
Instead of what I want to hear
To the man who encourages me through tears, shares my joy, holds
Me tight when I need strength
To the living being who keeps me safe and calm when I fear the world
I salute you, love you, need you with all my heart and mind
When darkness falls, I know my soul will search and cling to you
  - *From your charming wife*

McNamara's Band

I remember Dad playing 'McNamara's Band' on his brass trumpet, parading throughout the apartment, always studying his profile in our various mirrors.

He fancied himself a country singer, albeit never having left the tri-state area and possessing a thick Brooklyn accent. His campfire instrumental and singing skills were legendary…in his mind.

My three sisters and I did do a passable *'She'll be coming 'round the Mountain'* on the piano, with Dad on trumpet. Zayde would sing along. Zayde glanced in the mirror, but only to admire his beloved grandkids, Dad was focused only on his own reflection once having been told that he looked like Lloyd Nolan.

Do mirrors hold reflections, like our mind stores memories?

Our activities changed to stoop ball and Double Dutch jump rope.

We loved our Victrola. Each month we would buy a 45 rpm record of the top 20 hits and played it morning 'til bedtime weekends and after school.

We listened to songs of the 50s, while my Peter Pan dad did his own Modern dances, reducing us to guffaws and giggles. Dad was a fun-loving character, more of an older, irresponsible brother than father.

If I was to look in that old mirror, could I still see faded images of my sisters, Zayde and Dad?

I miss them still.

PART II

Tales of the Street

Observations from 2004-present as a volunteer at the Downtown San Diego Food Pantry

The Invisible Ones

Pastel on paper
By Margie November

Our Trash

Almost done bagel sandwich cream cheese raining over sides specks of
pink dried lox silver onion crushed in wax paper.
These are a few of their favorite things
Debris for recycle
Half empty lotion, half empty Vaseline
Used hairbrush, old scratched mismatched plates
Happy Birthday Mug with a missing handle
Slippers beaten down no longer snug,
Real leather belt with ripped hole
An apple slightly bruised a bit soft, same could be said for anyone of us.
this tasty.
I thoughtlessly discard.
Our recycle bin dumpster is a treasure trove for homeless denizens
Why look here's half a perfectly good sandwich, a half bottle of Tylenol
why it looks like Tylenol so what if way past date, I'm expired too.

Pay it Forward

He said, "pay it forward" asking for my blue backpack, "but what use will you give it?" I asked

He whipped out his student ID. He said "see I'm studying to be a teacher; I'll carry my books and papers. When I'm done with it, I'll pay it forward to another struggling student I'll pass it on to the children"

Am I a 'soft touch', a believer in second or third chances? Or am I a schmuck with a neon sign saying 'SUCKER'?

A woman I gave my denim jacket to is now a friend: Over the four years I've volunteered at the food bank, I've watched as her disease progressed and savaged her muscles. She went from a cane to being totally wheelchair bound. Backpack man may surprise me, who knows maybe he will be a teacher or counselor. As long as he becomes self-sufficient and pays it forward.

Hal

Donated food and sundries are distributed weekly at various venues downtown.

Every week a man pushes 'his home' to a different food site.

His 'home' rarely varies: it's an old shopping cart filled with yellowing newspapers, fabric scraps, torn blankets, a pair or two of mismatched shoes, tattered undefinable clothing. The home holds remnants of half eaten bagels or a roll. Occasionally half styrofoam cup of cooling dark coffee.

He could be anyone of the thousands of homeless on the streets of our country.

The Food Ladies call him Hal [no real names used at these distribution sites].

Over the last six months, Hal has been a regular at the various venues.

His age is undeterminable. He has the weathered skin of a man anywhere from his 50s to 70s.

He rarely takes the whole food bag: he has distinctive food preferences.

Hal is convinced of a government conspiracy against Homeless man, says food is not safe and only can eat coffee, soymilk, and of course chocolate.

He has become more friendly, helping the Food Ladies with heavy bags and occasionally serenading them.

The streets have been his home for over 20 years. At night, he sleeps in a relatively safe park under the lamp light with 'his buds'.

Says he has seen his buds die from cold, disease, drugs or at hands of "the crazies." He chose this life, but why? He doesn't want the offered shelters. Too many rules and a 10pm curfew.

Hal has become more than just another denizen of the homeless population, he is a Human Being hearing a very different tune.

A Home of Sorts

On the street so lonely and cold
Fearful of loss, pain and ill.
Wondering if anyone remembers him at home.
Home, smells of Thanksgiving turkey and pie, love and safety
Gone but the memories linger like a mist after rain hits the hot concrete
The man promised a clean bed hot showers and a toilet
Safe haven nice folk my check would be plenty- a room of my own.
Finally, a new beginning, possibilities a clean slate
Reality - the toilet works… mostly
Shower down the hall, door lock shoddy and shaky
My new neighbors are:
Bugs, drugs and thugs.

Homeless

Homeless ... in my mind, in my soul
A tornado came carrying me in its cortex
Away without my nest, away without a place
For my heart, for my breath.
Where are my stars and my sun?
Away from my mind, all gone.
Can I find a corner in His life that is mine?
In my soul in my heart:
A safe haven quiet and free.
A scrap of space I call my own?

Music Man

Tattered man dragging the remnants of his life stuffed in a Vons shopping cart
Overflowing with old books, yellowed music scores, assorted rags and tools.
All neatly topped with a cobbled together guitar.
Fondly touching the decrepit strings, he plucks a cord or two
Humming a tune known only to himself, lost in thoughts of good ole days.
Sixty years of memories contained in a metal wagon cloaked with dust, grease and tied with a shredded bungee
Told me he lives on the street, sleeps at the "Sally,"
code for Salvation Army.
"I used to teach music, I did in Illinois
Yes, I did."
Blue eyes twinkling, as if hearing sounds of music resonating in the classroom decades ago, now vanishing as in a mist. On his way to the "bird park" where music of pigeons replaces the once melodic sounds of happier times
He listens to the birds: his eyes closed as if in a concert hall,
Absentmindedly fondling his patchwork guitar. Does this instrument have a genetic memory of its once glorious time?

Book of Isiah

———— ❦ ————

At the food bank as I hand out the food.
I notice a weathered-face man could be 35 or 85
"What are you writing?" I asked him as I watched him enter numbers
"why, I'm studying Isiah," he responded
"Didn't know you read the bible, the old testament"
I've studied the Good book all my life, I have.
And a child shall lead them'
Slowly patiently he enters various numbers and jots a quote or two.
"Do you do this daily?"
"Oh yes, the good book offers many answers to daily life," said the man
whose whole life is bound by rags and faded papers and books.

When we chat, he's totally with me, mostly.
Then like a bolt of light shot him through his head
He talks argues, even pontificates
To no one in particular.

"Don't bother me, why are u pushing an old man, you're in error
You are in error, in error, sinner."

Shuffling back to the concrete wall, listening as he continues the rant
to the unseen participants. Then as quickly as it came, it's gone and he
exclaims:
"Here it is in the book, 'A child shall lead them. Isiah'!"

Every winter I die

"In the winter, l die..."
My little homeless friend told me this today
"Every winter I die, the birds die, I am cold so cold
all my coats blankets ain't helpin'"
I look into his clouded eyes, his shriveled face
"Can you go to Father Joes? I know there are clean beds, hot coffee
and warmth. I volunteer at the Rescue Mission, it's all good there," I
recommend

"NO! NO! I won't go again, I had to leave all my stuff outside, lost stuff,
they made me go to bed by 10 P.M. and there are rules, rules. Don't want
anyone's rules but mine."

"But it's dangerous out there, I worry about you if I don't see you for a
week," I said
"It is what it is," he responded
"Hey that's what grandpa used to say!" I exclaim
He repeats "every winter I die cold wet kills"
I gave him his bag plus the treats I get him, small towels, chocolate.
"You're an angel."
But it is what it is.
'Every winter I die,'

Weather and the Homeless:

A conversation of sorts about new storage containers for the homeless

Rain is rare, but when it happens
Gutters and streets flood
Our cozy store fronts and alleys are no longer.

When we have cloud grey, bone chilling days, it stinks
But, hell, our winter beats Minnesota, huh?

Maybe I'll seek shelter,
but losses happen.
Yeah, the Place has clean cots, toilets, hot coffee
but loss of my stuff, my carriage, my clothes, ...mine, mine

No, I won't leave my stuff, it's mine, the man always be stealing it,
touching it
telling me it's junk
No, it's not it is mine mine,
I'll get me more blankets maybe an old coat and papers

No way will I let them take my stuff
Spring will be here soon, park will warm up soon

if only I can be warm and dry with my stuff,
it's all I have, it's me.
So the man says
'72 hours to move all your stuff,
here's a plastic key we'll keep it safe'

Meryl Streep Doppelganger

I've watched as she morphed in reverse. A butterfly, a 'Meryl Streep clone' four years ago.
She holds her stately neck high and sits nursing a cup of coffee all day.
Using the restroom frequently... and increasingly longer stays.
Adding more cream and sugar as the coffee drains down in the cup.
She eats... nothing.
Talks silently to her friend, hidden in her mind.
Over the many months, she slowly enters more and more of a cocoon.
Her outward looks grow silently sullen and shallow.
Her hair and clothes more and more unkempt
Ignoring basic daily hygiene, her nails and teeth almost the same color
Once lovely coiffed hair in shambles and cascades of webbing and tangles, she is unaware.
Talking, not silently anymore, but in excited tones to her unseen friend.
She is angry and confused
Once, she had a job, wealth and a love
Now she struggles to meet simplest needs meals, clean bed .. clear mind
Silently her regal bearing carries her as she rides and drags her shopping cart and suitcase down the tangled narrow streets strewn with detritus of lives no different from her own
what caused her demise, was it drugs, booze or the warped tangles of her grey matter.
leading her to deteriorate in the daily view of others, from pristine princess to bag lady of bottom feeders.
she is Meryl Streep no longer.

PART III

Recipes

The ingredients of my love

Over the years that I've volunteered at the Food Pantry, I've wondered about their lives, especially their formative years.

Did Hal or Meryl have a crazy but loving Bubbe, Bubs, Zayde to guide them in the early years?

Was there a warmth and closeness between family members, did they share laughter,tears and food as I did with my early family?

Food is always a sign of love, caring, first aid, and always a cure for what ails you. If Bubs offered me Mandel bread (like biscotti) she never accepted refusal when I said I just ate, Bubs, she said…'whats that got to do with my mandelbroit'

Meals were shared as a family at least thru early high school years with some or/all sibs and adults.

Fridays was cleaning and preparation for the Shabbat meal. The Bubs would perfume the kitchen with smells of homemade soups, garlic-drenched ch ickens,kugels and challah bread. Bubs believe in Garlic. It was practically a wonder drug especially (when combined with chicken soup).

I was attempting to divine the mystery of ingredients: handful of this and that, pinch and touch of that. Seemly, magical, a finished product appeared. I tried to get recipes (ever the aspiring scientist and nutritionist). But Bubs kept the recipes locked in her brain.

I kept a sketchy journal of some of my favorites, hoping to duplicate a similar product for my future family.

INCLUDED IN The following section is some of Bubs' more memorable creations, as adopted by the pigtailed girl all grown up into her own Bubbe-ness.

Hoping that my kids and grandkids have memories of my Shabbat dinners, Breakfast at Bubbes(complete with menus) and special occasion Holiday FOODS. I've included a few for you dear readers to enjoy.

May our children and their children's children's lives and kitchens be filled with soul-satisfying foods, laughter, love and positive Bubbe memories.

Why recipes are optional

Bubs and I would cook and bake together
I was an eager, pigtailed eight-year-old
"Bubs, how much flour? How much water?" I would ask
"Handful of flour, a bissel* of water," Bubs would respond
Keep it going until it feels right
It's in the feel and smell
How many chilly afternoons did I come from ps 235?
To smells of years bread rising, chicken soup boiling, sometimes all over
the stove.
Mom taught school, Bubs cooked, baked and bossed
Zayde worked at the famous Grand Central Post Office
Recipe, schmeri, she'd say
It's in the feel and the smell…and taste

To this day, I follow her rules…or lack there of
Like the Bubs, it's either great…or not

*   a smidgen

Cup of Love From Me: And the Importance of Hot Tea

For healing or relaxing, Bubbe Abby says
Ginger, lemon and honey
Cinnamon, apple or berry tea
Soothe the sore throat, detox the world or calm a wild beast
Garlic keeps germs away…and most people
On cold, nasty Brooklyn days, when I was home with the flu, The Bubs would schlep hot chicken soup upstairs to me. The secret was rye toast slathered in garlic oil, plus plenty of hot Lipton's tea with lemon and honey.

Bubbe's Kosher Chicken Soup

Ingredients

1 quart of water
Chicken thighs
Add chopped carrots, onions, celery and 1 clove of garlic, season as desired
Put in the crock pot in the morning
Add more water as needed
At night – voila! Chicken soup!
For dinner – add quinoa, rice or matzo balls.

Bubbe's Refrigerator Overnight Oatmeal

Ingredients

1 cup steel cut oats
3 cups water or soymilk
Vanilla, cinnamon, raisins, walnuts and chopped apples, chopped and mixed together
Leave overnight in the fridge
Can be eaten hot or cold.

RoastedChickpeas

A nutritious and delicious snack that is high in protein

Ingredients

1 can low sodium chickpeas
2 tb olive oil
1 small chopped onion
2 tb garlic powder
½ c nutritional yeast

Instructions

Preheat oven to 400 degrees
Mix all ingredients
Place on a lightly sprayed or greased cookie sheet
Bake for 30-45 minutes or until a crispy, light brown

Dr.Bubbe's Nutritious Delicious Cheesecake (The Dr. Abby Modification)

Cheesecake often served during Shavuot commemorating getting The Ten Commandments at Mt. Sinai over 3,300 years ago. Not that I was there personally, perhaps my bubbe's bubbe…you get the point, was there. Needless to say: a long time ago.

Ingredients

1 graham cracker pie crust (low fat or homemade sugar free granola crust)
16 oz. 0% fat Greek yogurt, plain
2 oz. whipped cream cheese
2 oz. Stevia, sugar substitute
2 eggs
2 oz egg whites
2 tb vanilla
2 tb orange or lemon zest
1 tbsp OJ
½ cup unsweetened mini chocolate chips
¼ cup flour (use almond flour for gluten free)

Instructions

Preheat oven to 350 degrees
Mix together all dry ingredients
Slowly beat in eggs and other liquids (yogurt, cream cheese)
Slowly stir in chocolate chips
Pour in pie crust

Bake for 30-35 minutes or until top is golden brown
Cool top with ½ can of unsweetened cherry pie filling or ½ cup of crushed pineapple.

Veggie Frittata

Ingredients

4 eggs or 1 cup of egg whites – beaten
½ cup shredded skim milk mozzarella
½ cup drained spinach or broccoli
¼ cup shredded carrots
2 tsp garlic
½ cup chopped onion
¼ cup chopped red/green pepper
½ cup unsweetened, non-dairy milk

Instructions

Preheat oven to 350 degrees
Use a round, glass casserole dish (8 inches)
Spray casserole dish with oil
Mix together ingredients and pour into a greased dish
Bake for 30-40 minutes or until the eggs are set
Serve with salsa and Bloody Marys

PART IV

From this moment: My recipe

Transition 4/18/21

I am ageless in my soul
But not my body
Ageless in my heart…
But not my vitals
My heart glows…
with love and good vibes
Ageless in my smile.
not my discolored teeth.
No way is my spirit dissolving each time I wake.
I Thank God for each sunrise and sunset
No way do I complain of each snap, crackle and pop of my bones and
fascia .
Almost 8 revolutions around the sun
MY mirror reveals more cracks, whiskers, more scars, spots and wrinkles.
I have earned them all.
I thank the powers that be for the privilege of living…with tears, fears,
sorrow AND JOYS
With hugs and squeezes, whispers.
Soon I will be part of the great light of the world to come
I will miss my loved ones.
I left a piece of my soul in each of their hearts, which they will carry till
we meet again.

About the Author

Abby November was born in Brooklyn. After attending Hunter College and marrying, she completed her dietetic internship in Boston and earned a Master of Science in nutrition at the University of Wisconsin–Madison. Years later, November was awarded a PhD at New York University. She has performed stand-up since 1993 and currently resides in San Diego, California.

Printed in the United States
by Baker & Taylor Publisher Services